PAPER CRAFTS TUTORIALS!

PAPER PLANES, CUPS, DRAGONS AND MORE
CRAFTS FOR KIDS
CHILDREN'S CRAFT & HOBBY BOOKS

All Rights reserved. No part of this book may be reproduced or used in any way or form or by any means whether electronic or mechanical, this means that you cannot record or photocopy any material ideas or tips that are provided in this book

Copyright 2016

**What a crafty idea!
What else can you do with
a piece of paper?**

Kids, in this book you will learn easy-to-follow steps for turning a piece of paper into almost anything. The products are pretty cool and artistic!

The universal medium for writing is pen and paper. As years passed by, people have discovered some creative ways to use papers apart from writing.

PAPER PLANE

Take one whole sheet of paper and fold it in half. Open the paper again to lay it flat. Second, the **cockpit** will be folded at the center. Third, fold the **cockpit** down so that the point lines up with the center fold line.

Fold the second cockpit by folding the tow flaps the same way as in the second step. To make it look really like an airplane, make another two folds for the wings. Your airplane is now ready to take off!

PAPER DRAGON

First, create a beginner level dragon. Consider starting with a big sheet of paper. Begin with a square piece of paper and fold the paper in half by folding the top corner to the bottom corner. Fold the triangle in half by meeting the left and right corners.

Open and spread the top flap. Crease the left and right sides. Make the left flap vertically, then open it and squash it down. Then fold the top layers of both sides to the centers. Then fold the top triangle down.

Make the kite-fold. The right and left corners are folded into the center diagonal line. Start from the top corner. Then make pleats on each side of the diamond by turning the paper over and bring the new side corners again to the center from the bottom corner.

Open the paper and repeat these folds from the top corner. Then, fold along the other diagonal. After this, pinch the corners together into a pleated diamond. Fold the bottom corner to the top corner along the center diagonal. Bring the left corner up in between the two layers.

Using another reverse-fold on the left side, make the head. To create the mouth, bring the left corner down to the right along a diagonal and then back right along a diagonal. Then, fold the wings down and open them to the sides. Now the dragon is finished.

PAPER GLASS

We can make a pretty paper glass from coffee filters. How is it done? Just follow these simple procedures and be amazed at this crafty idea.

Trim the edge of a coffee filter to make an uneven organic shape. Use non-permanent markers to make lines, spots and blobs on the coffee filter.

Drape the coffee filter over a plastic cup. Then, apply spray starch to the filter, letting the color mix and bleed together. Finally, let the filter dry and enjoy your paper glass.

PAPER BOAT

First, fold the paper in half. Then take the two folded corners and bring them in the center.

Next, fold the excess edges over the folded corners and to the other side. Finally, to have the cone at the center stick up, fold out the edges of the paper.

Then, add volume to your boat by sticking your fingers into this cone. The edges around it are folded.

PAPER CUP

First, have your paper white side up. Fold it in half. Then fold the top corner down to the baseline. Crease well and unfold. After this, fold the bottom left hand corner up to the crease line. Fold the bottom right hand corner up to the opposite side.

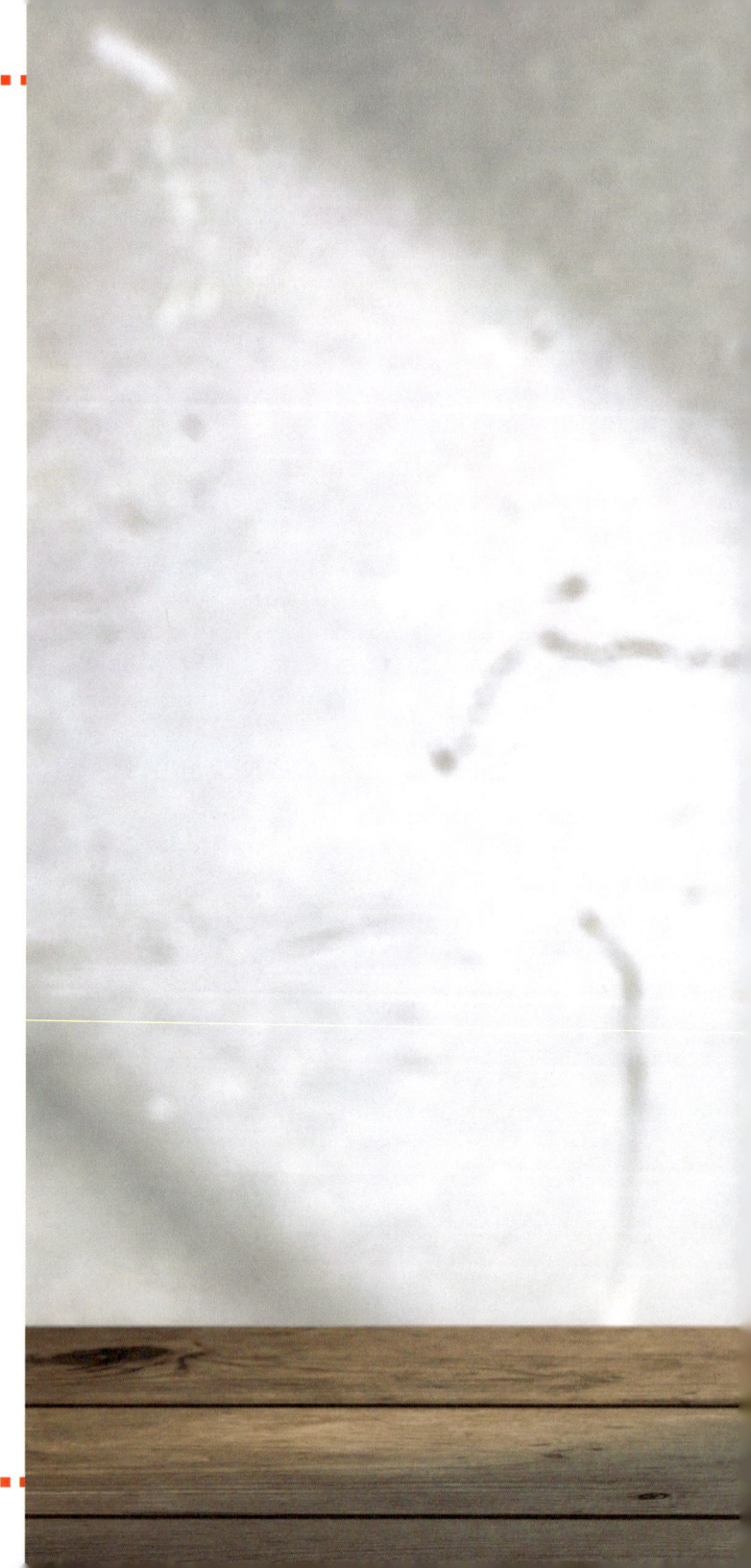

Then, fold the front flap downwards. Next, fold the back top flap backwards. Finally, open everything out. Your drinking cup is done!

This simple craft can make the world of kids an exciting and enjoyable one. Every piece of paper has its use. So make use of them.

www.ingramcontent.com/pod-product-compliance
Lightning Source LLC
LaVergne TN
LVRC090218080426
835507LV00038B/148